improving
communication
in your marriage

homebuilders
COUPLES SERIES®

improving
communication
in your marriage

by
dr. gary & barbara
rosberg

FAMILYLIFE®
Little Rock, Arkansas

IMPROVING COMMUNICATION IN YOUR MARRIAGE
FamilyLife Publishing®
5800 Ranch Drive
Little Rock, Arkansas 72223
1-800-FL-TODAY • FamilyLife.com

FLTI, d/b/a FamilyLife®, is a ministry of Campus Crusade for Christ International®

ISBN: 978-1-60200-332-3

Design: Brand Navigation, LLC

Cover image: © Getty Images/Visual Ideas/Nora Pelaez

Printed in the United States of America

17 16 15 14 13   5 6 7 8 9

FAMILYLIFE®

Unless the Lord builds the house,
those who build it labor in vain.

<small>PSALM</small> 127:1

The HomeBuilders Couples Series®

The HomeBuilders Parenting Series®

Marriage should be enjoyed, not endured. It is meant to be a vibrant relationship between two people who love each other with passion, commitment, understanding, and grace. So secure is the bond God desires between a husband and a wife that he uses it to illustrate the magnitude of Christ's love for the church (Ephesians 5:25–33).

Do you have that kind of love in your marriage?

Relationships often fade over time as people drift apart—but only if the relationship is left unattended. We have a choice in the matter; our marriages don't have to grow dull. Perhaps we just need to give them some attention.

That's the purpose behind the HomeBuilders Couples Series®— to provide you a way to give your marriage the attention it needs and deserves. This is a biblically based small-group study because, in the Bible, God has given the blueprint for building a loving and secure marriage. His plan is designed to enable a man and a woman to grow together in a mutually satisfying relationship and then to reach out to others with the love of Christ. Ignoring God's plan may lead to isolation and, in far too many cases, the breakup of the home.

Whether your marriage needs a complete makeover or just a few small adjustments, we encourage you to consult God's design. Although written nearly two thousand years ago, Scripture still speaks clearly and powerfully about the conflicts and challenges men and women face.

Do we really need to be part of a group? Couldn't we just go through this study as a couple?

While you could work through the study as a couple, you would miss the opportunity to connect with friends and to learn from one another's experiences. You will find that the questions in each session not only help you grow closer to your spouse, but they also create an environment of warmth and fellowship with other couples as you study together.

What does it take to lead a HomeBuilders group?

Leading a group is much easier than you may think, because the leader is simply a facilitator who guides the participants through the discussion questions. You are not teaching the material but are helping the couples discover and apply biblical truths. The special dynamic of a HomeBuilders group is that couples teach themselves.

The study guide you're holding has all the information and guidance you need to participate in or lead a HomeBuilders group. You'll find leader's notes in the back of the guide, and additional helps are posted online at FamilyLife.com/Resources.

What is the typical schedule?

Most studies in the HomeBuilders Couples Series are six to eight weeks long, indicated by the number of sessions in the guide. The sessions are designed to take sixty minutes in the group with a project for the couples to complete between sessions.

Isn't it risky to talk about your marriage in a group?

The group setting should be enjoyable and informative—and non-threatening. THREE SIMPLE GROUND RULES will help ensure that everyone feels comfortable and gets the most out of the experience:

1. Share nothing that will embarrass your spouse.
2. You may pass on any question you do not want to answer.
3. If possible, as a couple complete the HomeBuilders project between group sessions.

What other help does FamilyLife offer?

Our list of marriage and family resources continues to grow. Visit FamilyLife.com to learn more about our:

- Weekend to Remember® getaway, The Art of Marriage®, and other events;
- slate of radio broadcasts, including the nationally syndicated *FamilyLife Today*®, *Real FamilyLife with Dennis Rainey*®, and *FamilyLife This Week*®;
- multimedia resources for small groups, churches, and community networking;
- interactive products for parents, couples, small-group leaders, and one-to-one mentors; and
- assortment of blogs, forums, and other online connections.

Dr. Gary and Barbara Rosberg are award-winning authors and popular radio hosts and marriage-conference speakers. Together they cofounded the national ministry America's Family Coaches. Through a unique process called "The Great Marriage Experience," the Rosbergs equip couples and churches with the resources, events, and tools they need to keep their marriages growing stronger for a lifetime.

contents

Polls and surveys consistently show that communication is the number one issue crippling a married couple's relationship. And it doesn't take much time for this problem to show itself. Once those feelings of hyper-romance from dating and engagement begin to fade, married couples often wake up to some cold realizations: We aren't talking the way we once did. We're having more disagreements than we ever thought we would. And we don't know how to handle it.

In this study you will learn how to improve your communication—how to talk to each other, how to listen, how to "close the loop" in conflict, and much more. And you'll have fun learning, because you'll do it with other couples who face the same issues in their marriages.

We can't think of any better guides in this process than Gary and Barbara Rosberg. They know that the principles in this study work—they've seen them transform their marriage, and they've seen them influence thousands to have the kind of relationship God desires for a married couple.

Our prayer is that this study will launch you on a journey that will never end—a journey toward oneness in your marriage.

—Dennis & Barbara Rainey

1 Understanding the Barriers to Communication

Building a healthy marriage requires strong communication; strong communication requires an understanding of the things that interfere.

Married Mishaps

Introduce yourselves as a couple by briefly answering one or both of the following questions (remember, don't share anything negative or embarrassing):

- What is one difference in you and your spouse that you're both able to laugh about?

- What's the funniest miscommunication you've heard of in someone's marriage in real life, on TV, or in a movie?

Any two people in a relationship will face barriers in communicating effectively. Overcoming these barriers is part of the challenge of marriage. Unfortunately, many couples have never taken the time to understand the barriers they face.

The Number One Need

1. Couples everywhere indicate that the biggest need in their marriages is improved communication. Why is good communication so difficult?

2. Why do you think good communication is vital to a healthy marriage?

 homebuilders principle: How well you communicate can make or break your marriage.

Barriers to Communication

3. One common barrier in marriage is differing styles of communication. What are some general differences in the way men and women communicate? In the way introverted and extroverted individuals communicate?

4. Another common barrier to communication is the pressure of a busy lifestyle. How does this kind of pressure sometimes make it difficult to communicate with each other?

5. We all learn how to communicate—and how *not* to communicate—by observing the behavior of others. The most enduring lessons in communication usually come from our parents. What did your parents do *well* in communicating with each other? What did they *not* do well? If you were not raised by both parents, focus on whoever raised you.

6. What barriers to good communication have you adopted from your parents' example?

Communication Barriers and the Bible

7. Even Jesus experienced barriers to communication. Read Luke 10:38–42. What kept Martha from hearing Jesus' message? What was Jesus' solution to Martha's problem?

PICTURE THIS

Stand facing your spouse and think of something that happened today that you'd like to tell your spouse. Before you start to speak, hold your open book directly between you so you can't see each other's face. Take one minute to tell your spouse what happened, without moving the book away. Then switch, and with the same barrier in place, have your spouse take one minute to tell you about something that happened today. After the two minutes are up, talk with the whole group about the following questions:

- How did it feel to have a barrier between you when you were trying to share with each other?
- How does this exercise illustrate the way barriers to communication hinder marriage relationships?

8. Read Ephesians 4:11–16. What does this passage say about the connection between appropriate communication and spiritual maturity?

9. What does it mean to speak "the truth in love"?

homebuilders principle: Effective communication with your spouse requires truthfulness and openness.

make a date

Set a time for you and your spouse to complete the HomeBuilders project together before the next group meeting. You will be asked at the next session to share an insight or experience from the project.

date _____ time _____

location _____

homebuilders project

On Your Own

Answer the following questions:

1. What one insight have you gained about the communication within your marriage from this session?

2. What barriers do you and your spouse face in communication?

3. On the following scale, evaluate your own communication strengths and weaknesses by circling the appropriate number.

	Never			Sometimes				Often		
Verbally express love	1	2	3	4	5	6	7	8	9	10
Listen sincerely and attentively	1	2	3	4	5	6	7	8	9	10
Talk too much	1	2	3	4	5	6	7	8	9	10
Talk through problems	1	2	3	4	5	6	7	8	9	10
Discuss situations logically	1	2	3	4	5	6	7	8	9	10
Share intimately	1	2	3	4	5	6	7	8	9	10
Share goals and dreams	1	2	3	4	5	6	7	8	9	10
Give nonsexual touch	1	2	3	4	5	6	7	8	9	10
Provide encouragement	1	2	3	4	5	6	7	8	9	10
Address conflict appropriately	1	2	3	4	5	6	7	8	9	10
Avoid addressing conflict	1	2	3	4	5	6	7	8	9	10
Honestly express emotions	1	2	3	4	5	6	7	8	9	10

With Your Spouse

1. Share with each other your answers from the individual time. Discuss your perceptions of how accurately your spouse rated his or her communication strengths and weaknesses.

2. How easy is it to face up to your own barriers to effective communication? Why?

3. In what ways do you complement each other in your strengths and weaknesses in communication?

4. What areas would you like to improve during this Home-Builders study?

5. What is one thing you can do next week to overcome a barrier to communication?

6. Spend time in prayer, confessing sin to God as needed. Ask him for guidance, wisdom, and power in improving your communication. Ask God to help you help each other overcome barriers to communication.

Remember to take your calendar to the next session for Make a Date.

2

Making Your Relationship a Priority

To develop positive communication patterns, you must make your marriage relationship a priority.

A Modern Stone-Age Family

Read the following case study, and discuss what thoughts might fill in the blanks.

Wilma was getting fed up. Every night Fred came home from a hard day at the quarry and plopped in front of the TV to watch Championship Rock Wrestling. He barely uttered a grunt the whole evening except for the noises he made while chowing down the brontosaurus ribs Wilma had prepared. Fred often ignored Pebbles and left Wilma to bear the brunt of the cavework and parenting chores. Wilma was so tired at night that she usually was asleep before Fred came to bed. Finally Wilma was ready to explode, and one Saturday she confronted Fred.

Fill in the blanks:

Wilma said: _____

Fred responded: _____

Wilma countered: _____

Fred said: _____

Now discuss the following questions:

- What kinds of communication problems are Fred and Wilma experiencing?

- How have their priorities affected their communication? Their relationship?

- How could they improve their communication?

Project Report

If you completed the HomeBuilders project from the first session, share one thing you learned.

blueprints

A relationship is a living thing; it thrives with attention and withers when ignored. To maintain a healthy relationship, married couples should regularly examine how they spend their most precious resources—their time and energy—and determine whether they are following their priorities. Many couples find that each anniversary is a good time to evaluate priorities together.

Your Most Precious Resources

1. What pressures in your life make it a challenge for you to give your marriage the time and energy it needs to grow stronger?

2. How do the following passages relate to making your marriage and home a priority?

    * Ephesians 5:15–16

- Philippians 2:1–4

- Song of Solomon 7:10–13

3. What good examples of making a marriage relationship a priority have you seen modeled by other couples?

Personalizing Your Marriage Priorities

4. What things have you done lately to make your relationship a priority?

5. What barriers do you face in taking time with your spouse every day?

6. What could you change in your normal daily schedule to make more room for your relationship?

7. What fun, creative dates have you had together since you were married? What impact have they had on your relationship?

Focusing Your Attention

8. Suppose you were able to take the attention you normally give to your work and transfer it to your family instead. What would that do to your family? What would that do to your work?

9. Since transferring *all* your attention from work to your family is likely impossible, what are some ways you *could* give more attention to your home life?

homebuilders principle: For communication within a marriage to be effective, you must reserve time and energy for your spouse.

make a date

Set a time for you and your spouse to complete the HomeBuilders project together before the next group meeting. You will be asked at the next session to share an insight or experience from the project.

date _____ time _____

location _____

homebuilders project

On Your Own

Answer the following questions:

1. What insight about communication in marriage have you gained from this session?

2. How do you feel about the amount of time and energy you are saving each day for your spouse? For your children?

3. Evaluate:

   - Within the last month, have you let a day get so full that you barely had time to say "good morning" and "good night" to your spouse?
   - Have you recently ignored your spouse—even for a minute—because you were watching television?
   - Within the last year, have you let work replace a time that the two of you had planned to spend together?
   - Within the last six months, have you let a dispute over children, friends, or activities go unresolved and come between you?

- Have you ever let a hobby or other interest consume so much of you that your spouse felt neglected?

4. If you changed your priorities, what differences do you think that would make in your relationship and communication with your spouse?

5. How do you feel about the amount of time and energy your spouse saves each day for you? For your children?

6. If you received more of your spouse's time and energy, what difference might that make in your life?

With Your Spouse

1. Share at least one example of a time you thought your spouse really made your marriage a priority.

2. Share your responses to the questions you answered on your own.

3. What would be a good time each day to devote to talking to each other? Even if you start with just ten minutes, set a time and stick with it.

4. What changes would you need to make—and what obstacles would you need to overcome—to spend this time together?

5. Pray together, committing to God to make your marriage a higher priority this week.

Remember to take your calendar to the next session for Make a Date.

3

Communication 101

Learning to use basic communication skills will enhance understanding within your marriage.

At First Sight

Tell the group about one or two things you saw in your future spouse while you were dating that led you to think, "This is the person I want to marry."

Project Report

If you completed the HomeBuilders project from the last session, share one thing you learned.

blueprints

Just because words are being spoken does not mean that real communication is taking place. For solid communication with understanding to occur, three components must be present: expressing, listening, and responding.

1. Read Proverbs 16:16 and 24:3. Why do you think "understanding" is important to a good marriage relationship?

The First Component: Expressing

When you talk with someone, you want that person to understand what you are saying and feeling. You want to be understood. Clear communication involves deliberate expression. In order for your spouse to understand you, talk openly about what you *think*, what you *feel*, and what you *need* in the current situation.

2. Remember that you are using an incredibly powerful tool—the tongue. Read James 3:3–12. According to this passage, what is dangerous about the tongue? Tell the group about a criticism or cutting comment that you remember from years ago. How did it affect you? (Do *not* tell a comment from your marriage.)

3. According to James 3:3–12, what's *good* about the tongue? Tell the group about an encouragement or compliment you received years ago that you've never forgotten. How did it affect you?

The Second Component: Listening

4. Read James 1:19. Why is it good to be "quick to hear" and "slow to speak"? What does it take to be a good listener?

5. Think of two or three good listeners you know. How do you feel about spending time with them? Why do you feel this way?

Listening isn't always easy. Often we want to jump in and give advice or fix the other person's problem. However, listening carefully is a key to understanding your spouse's true needs. When a person is talking, he or she needs to be "in the spotlight." Each person needs the time and freedom for full expression without interruption or feedback.

Unfortunately, the one who is listening often wants to grab the spotlight, thus short-circuiting the communication process. When two or more people constantly fight for the spotlight, caring only about expressing themselves, communication breaks down.

6. With your spouse, take turns being in the spotlight. When it's your turn, spend about two to three minutes talking to your spouse about a problem you currently are experiencing *outside of your marriage relationship*. The problem could be at work, at home with a child, with a neighbor, or with a family member. Tell your spouse what you think and feel about the situation and what you need from him or her. Be careful not to direct any criticism toward your spouse, and when it's your turn to listen, don't interrupt.

For extra impact: Gather enough flashlights so that each couple has one. Lower the lights in the meeting room, and have one spouse shine the spotlight on the other while it's his or her turn to talk. After both of you have been in the spotlight, discuss the following question within your group.

7. How did you feel when you were the one talking? How did you feel as you were listening?

The Third Component: Responding

At some point in most conversations, you need to move beyond listening. You need to join the conversation and seek to truly understand what your spouse is saying. You can do that by responding with appropriate feedback.

8. What kinds of inappropriate responses do we sometimes give that don't promote better understanding?

9. What are some appropriate types of feedback that lead to better understanding? How does appropriate feedback help build an environment of openness and trust in your communication?

Your spouse needs to know that you are committed to him or her. You want to make the relationship work. You want to listen, and you want to help. One simple feedback question will communicate this if stated sincerely: "What do you need most from me right now?"

At times your spouse may ask you to suggest a solution to a problem. At other times he or she may just need you to listen. Your responsibility is to be sincerely interested and ready to respond with what your spouse needs.

homebuilders principle: You can foster positive communication in your marriage by using basic communication skills— expressing, listening, and responding.

The basic components of communication may sound simple, but mastering them is a lifelong challenge. Like any new skill, they require lots of practice. But the important thing is to get started and keep at it. Your first few attempts at changing your communication patterns may be less than perfect, but keep trying. The eventual results will be well worth any initial difficulties.

make a date

Set a time for you and your spouse to complete the HomeBuilders project together before the next group meeting. You will be asked at the next session to share an insight or experience from the project.

date _____ time _____

location _____

homebuilders project

On Your Own

Answer the following questions:

1. What were your most significant insights from this week's session?

2. On a scale of 1 (poor) to 5 (excellent), how would you rate yourself as a clear communicator? As a sincere listener? As an appropriate responder?

3. On a scale of 1 (poor) to 5 (excellent), how would you rate your spouse as a clear communicator? As a sincere listener? As an appropriate responder?

4. What do you appreciate about your spouse's conversation skills?

5. What do you need to improve the most in your communication skills?

6. What is one concern in your marriage that you'd like to discuss with your spouse?

With Your Spouse

1. Tell your spouse about something he or she said to you that you really appreciated.

2. Discuss the first five questions that you each answered on your own. Be open, kind, and understanding as you address difficult issues.

3. Tell each other about the concerns you listed under question 6. Tackle those concerns one at a time, using the components of communication learned in this week's session. Be sure to speak, listen, and respond only at the appropriate times. Follow the steps even if it feels awkward. It will become more natural with practice. When it's your time to

give feedback, ask questions to help clarify your understanding. Summarize what you think you heard, and ask if you understood correctly. Before you leave each concern, be sure to ask, "What do you need most from me right now?"

4. Wrap up your time together with prayer, committing to practice good communication skills within your marriage in the coming weeks.

Remember to take your calendar to the next session for Make a Date.

4

Closing the Loop in Conflict

Resolving conflict requires taking initiative to mend the relationship.

warm-up

Minor Irritations

Conflict is inevitable when two people live together. In his book *Staying Close,* Dennis Rainey lists a number of seemingly small things that can spark arguments and conflicts. Tell the group about one of these that caused a now-humorous conflict in your marriage. Or tell about a different one that stands out in your mind.

- Sleeping in the dark or with a night light on
- Leaving windows open or closed
- Where to set the house thermostat
- How to eat
- How to blow your nose

- What kind of music to play on the stereo
- How loud the music is played
- Where clothing is placed after it's taken off
- The way to hang toilet paper
- What time to go to bed or to get up
- Whether the cap is kept on the toothpaste tube
- Whether cupboard doors are closed
- Who makes the bed and how
- Who locks the doors at night

Project Report

Share one thing you learned from the HomeBuilders project from last session.

blueprints

When you put two people together in marriage, conflict is inevitable. The differences between men and women alone ensure many areas of disagreement. On top of that, people come from different backgrounds, enjoy different hobbies and interests, and relate to others in different ways. Though couples may manage to ignore their differences during courtship and engagement, eventually the glow wears off, and they encounter conflict.

1. Why do you think so many couples are not adept at resolving conflict in marriage?

God delights in restoring broken relationships. In seeking to help couples rebuild relationships, Dr. Rosberg has identified a common sequence of events in most conflicts. Each time a conflict begins, a loop is formed, and that loop is closed only when the conflict is resolved. "Closing the loop" is what we want to see happen. More information on this concept can be found in *Dr. Rosberg's Do-It-Yourself Relationship Mender.*

The Loop Opens

A typical conflict begins with an *offense*—one spouse does something that offends the other. That spouse is usually *hurt* by the offense, and the hurt often gives way to *anger.*

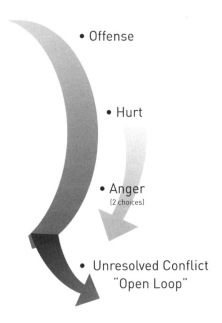

- Offense

- Hurt

- Anger
  (2 choices)

- Unresolved Conflict
  "Open Loop"

Case Study: Quiche Again?

Sue works about six hours a day while the couple's three children are in school. On a typical afternoon she arrives home at 3:30 and then heads out to take the children to basketball practice and piano lessons. She returns home at 5:30 just before her husband, Brian, arrives from his own day at work.

Brian finds Sue in the kitchen, starting dinner for the family. He looks at the counter and says, "We're having quiche *again*? I'm getting tired of that stuff. Can't you come up with anything else?"

"Hey, I don't see you at work in the kitchen, do I?" Sue responds angrily. "I'm tired of your complaining about my cooking. I'd be glad to have you take over anytime you want!"

2. Put yourself in Sue's shoes. How would she feel when she hears Brian's comment?

3. How does anger affect a person's response in a conflict?

Open or Closed

At this point in a conflict, you come to a critical choice: Do you resolve the conflict or let it pass? Do you close the loop or leave it open?

4. What might keep Brian and Sue from taking the initiative to resolve their conflict?

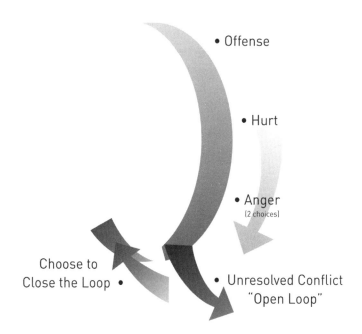

• Offense

• Hurt

• Anger
(2 choices)

Choose to
Close the Loop •

• Unresolved Conflict
"Open Loop"

5. What happens in a marriage relationship when conflicts are left unresolved?

6. What do the following verses say about closing the loop and resolving conflict?

- Matthew 18:21–22

- Ephesians 4:26–27

homebuilders principle: You should seek to resolve conflict so that your marriage relationship is not damaged.

Closing the Loop

Step one: preparing your heart

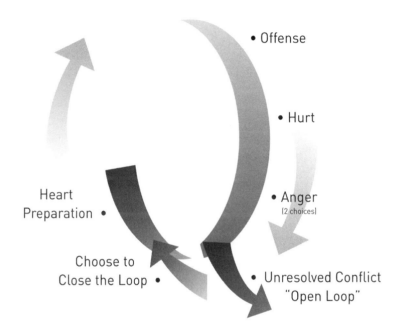

7. What guidance do the following passages offer for preparing your heart to resolve a conflict?

- Psalm 139:23–24

- 1 Peter 3:8–9

homebuilders principle: Resolving conflict requires humility.

Step two: loving confrontation

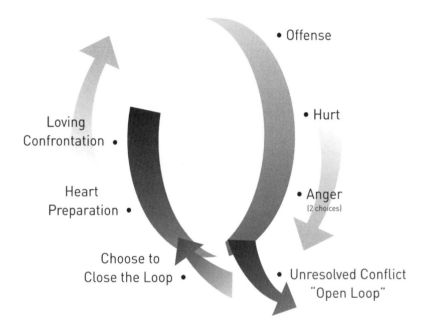

• Offense

• Hurt

Loving
Confrontation •

• Anger
(2 choices)

Heart
Preparation •

Choose to
Close the Loop •

• Unresolved Conflict
"Open Loop"

In this step you discuss the conflict with your spouse. It's important to use the components of good communication that were discussed in the last session. For example, focus on listening to your spouse rather than doing all the talking yourself. Look for a resolution that benefits both of you. Also, be sure to choose the right time and place to discuss the conflict.

8. In your relationship why are certain times better than others for working through a conflict?

Step three: offering forgiveness

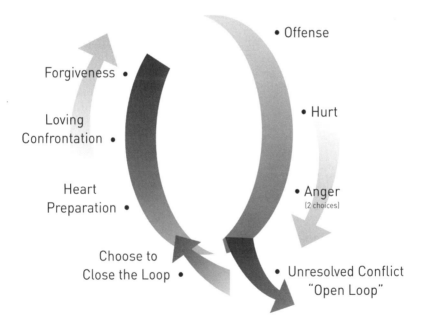

- Offense
- Hurt
- Anger
  (2 choices)
- Unresolved Conflict
  "Open Loop"

Forgiveness •

Loving
Confrontation •

Heart
Preparation •

Choose to
Close the Loop •

Forgiveness is vital to closing the loop in a relationship. Without it, you're trapped by anger; you'll never know the reconciliation of two hearts that once again are tender toward each other.

9. Read Ephesians 4:32. What does it mean to forgive others just as God in Christ forgave you? Why is it so difficult to do?

homebuilders principle: Forgiveness is the key element in resolving conflict.

Step four: rebuilding trust

Case Study Follow-up: More Quiche?

After a loving confrontation, Brian realizes he's been too hard on Sue about cooking meals when she's as busy as he is. He asks for her forgiveness and promises to help out more at dinnertime—and not to complain about what she fixes.

10. If you were Sue, would you now trust Brian to quit complaining and handle his part of preparing dinner? Why or why not? What must he do to rebuild her trust?

homebuilders principle: Forgiving your spouse does not always mean that you will automatically *trust* him or her; trust takes time to rebuild.

For extra impact: If you have time, read the following case study and complete the exercise.

During eight years of marriage, Sheila has repeatedly mishandled her family's finances. She has not kept a good record of what is in the checking account, and she has spent freely. As a result, she and her husband, Darrin, have a growing debt and a bad credit record. They just had a new-car loan denied, and Darrin is very angry.

Walk through each of the steps presented in this session, suggesting what could be said and done at each step to close the loop.

Step One: Preparing Your Heart

Step Two: Loving Confrontation

Step Three: Offering Forgiveness

Step Four: Rebuilding Trust

Share with the group the most important thing you've learned from this session about handling conflict.

make a date

Set a time for you and your spouse to complete the HomeBuilders project together before the next group meeting. You will be asked at the next session to share an insight or experience from the project.

date _____ time _____

location _____

homebuilders project

On Your Own

1. Review the material from the Blueprints section. What are
    some of the main things you learned during the session?

2. Do you ever find yourself getting stuck at a certain stage in
    the conflict-resolution process? Why?

3. What do you personally need to work on in your conflict-
    resolution skills?

4. What conflict have you faced in your marriage relationship
    during the past month?

5. At what stage in the closing-the-loop sequence do you currently find yourselves in this conflict?

6. What do you (not your spouse) need to do to work toward resolution?

With Your Spouse

1. Go through the first three questions that you answered on your own, and share your answers.

2. Work through questions 4–6, approaching each conflict (from question 4) separately. Begin by praying together, asking God to give you humility, insight, and wisdom as you discuss the conflict and how to resolve it. Be sure to follow the steps to closing the loop on conflict.

Remember to take your calendar to the next session for Make a Date.

5 Communicating Through the Trials of Life

God can use you to encourage your spouse during times of trial.

warm-up

Typical Trials

Discuss the following questions.

What typical struggles or trials does a couple face when

- they're newly married?
- they have their first baby?
- they try to create and live by a budget?
- they move hundreds of miles from home?
- they have a teenager in the house?
- old age sets in?

Project Report

Share one thing you learned from the HomeBuilders project from last session.

Anticipating the Trials

In 1995 an American F-16 fighter jet was shot down in enemy terrain over northern Bosnia. Six days later its pilot, Scott O'Grady, was rescued by a Marine helicopter team. Americans were fascinated by O'Grady's story—how he ate insects, captured rainwater to ease his thirst, and narrowly evaded Bosnian search teams.

O'Grady's survival was a testament to his Air Force training. He had completed a seventeen-day survival school where he learned to live off the land and to maintain a positive mental attitude. When he left on his mission, he wore a survival vest packed with equipment. Even his seat, which ejected with him, contained invaluable equipment. O'Grady was prepared for his ordeal. He knew what to do when the trials came.

Trials are an inevitable part of life. Scott O'Grady was able to handle six days on his own in hostile territory. Yet few people are prepared to handle the unavoidable storms of life.

1. Read James 1:2–4. Notice that James writes about "when" trials come, not "if" they come. Why are so few people prepared to handle trials and challenges?

2. What typically happens in a marriage relationship when trials hit?

3. How has your marriage relationship been affected by trials and stresses?

homebuilders principle: As a couple you must be prepared for the trials that will inevitably occur during your life together.

Preparing for the Trials

4. Look ahead to the next twenty to thirty years of your mar-

Discuss questions 4 and 5 with your spouse. When you're done, you may want to share an appropriate insight or discovery with the group.

riage. What trials and stresses are you likely to face at some point (examples: death of parents, adjustments to in-laws)?

5. How do you expect these trials to affect your relationship?

Turning to God in the Trials of Life

6. What does each of the following passages say about why God allows trials and suffering?

- Romans 8:28

- 1 Peter 1:3–9

- 1 Peter 4:12–14

7. Describe something good that came out of a trial you faced.

8. Read the following passages. How have you seen the truth of one of these scriptures in your life?

- 1 Corinthians 10:13

- 2 Corinthians 1:3–4

- Philippians 4:12–13

9. Read Philippians 4:6–7. What does this passage say about *how* we're to face the trials of our lives? Describe a situation where you needed God's peace.

homebuilders principle: You and your spouse can help each other persevere and even experience joy during trials by encouraging each other and pointing each other to God.

make a date

Set a time for you and your spouse to complete the HomeBuilders project together before the next group meeting. You will be asked at the next session to share an insight or experience from the project.

date _____ time _____

location _____

homebuilders project

On Your Own

1. Look over your notes from the session, and write down the key insights you gained.

2. As you look back on your marriage, how would you evaluate your success at dealing with the trials you've faced so far? What were the reasons for your success or lack of success?

3. What trials are you facing right now? How can your spouse help you deal with them? How can God help you?

4. Some people tend to pull away from their spouses during difficult times, but God intends that spouses support each other in trials. Every couple needs to make a conscious commitment to work through trials together.

Once you've made that commitment, the following four principles will help you communicate during trials in such a way that you build up each other. These principles can revolutionize your marriage if you practice them. Read each principle, and answer the question following it with your spouse.

- *Determine what you need from each other.* The easiest way to learn this is just to ask each other on a regular basis, "What do you need from me right now?"

- *Determine to face the problem head-on together.* Often we hope the pain will go away if we focus on other things or if we fill our hours with activities. It won't work—the pain must be faced.

- *Point each other to God.* Pray together as a couple. Read Scripture to each other. (Psalms 23, 31, and 34 are good selections.) Maintain your relationship to God as his child, and help your spouse do the same.

- *Seek help from friends and family.* As a couple you may be tempted to isolate yourself from your children, friends, and family in a time of trial. Instead, admit your need, and allow the body of Christ to fulfill its function in supporting you.

5. To what extent do you lean on God and your spouse during times of stress and suffering? What can you do to improve?

With Your Spouse

1. Recall a trial you experienced as a couple. Share with each
    other what you gained and learned from that trial.

2. Look over the points from question 4. How can you apply
    these principles to a situation in your life right now? Decide
    on and commit to three ways you'll begin applying the
    principles of this session to your lives during the next week.
    Gently hold each other accountable for following through on
    your commitments.

3. Close your time in prayer. If you're going through trials right
    now, use the verses from the Blueprints section to guide you
    in prayer. Ask God to give you joy during these trials, and
    pray that you will be an encouragement to each other.

Remember to take your calendar to the next session for Make a Date.

6

Achieving
Spiritual Intimacy

The best and deepest level of communication is
achieved when you seek God together.

warm-up

Moving Forward

As you come to the end of this study, reflect as a group on what you
have experienced. Pick one of the following questions to answer,
and share with the group.

- What has this group meant to you during the course of
  this study? Be specific.
- What is the most valuable thing you discovered?
- What would you like to see happen next for this group?
- How have you changed as a result of what you've learned
  in this study?

Project Report

Share one thing you learned from the HomeBuilders project from last session.

blueprints

Many of the principles we've discussed for better communication within marriage could be applied just as well by non-Christians. You don't have to be a believer in Jesus Christ to make time for your spouse, to save energy for when you get home, or to close the loop in conflicts. But a truly Christian marriage will be different from any other.

1. What do you think should make a Christian marriage—and communication within that marriage—distinctive?

The Best Part of Marriage

Spiritual intimacy is one ingredient of marriage that is available only to those who have a personal relationship with God through Jesus Christ and who live their lives seeking to please him. When both a husband and wife are growing in their vertical relationships with God, the horizontal relationship between them tends to come together as well. This is the best part of marriage.

2. Read Acts 4:31–32. How did the Christians relate to one another after they had been filled with the Holy Spirit? What do you think it means to be "of one heart and soul"?

3. Read Colossians 3:12–17. If you as "God's chosen ones" let the "peace of Christ rule in your hearts," how will that affect your marriage relationship?

4. What kinds of actions and experiences will lead toward deeper spiritual intimacy with your spouse?

homebuilders principle: Truly intimate communication comes only when as a couple you seek God and let him knit your hearts together.

Taking Action

Many Christian couples wish they would spend more time together praying and reading the Word of God. They know what they should do, but they don't do it. A typical comment is, "I know we should have more of a spiritual life together, and I want that, but we just don't ever seem to get around to doing anything about it."

Some couples simply have never built into their lives the discipline of spending time together with God. If you've been faithful in completing the HomeBuilders projects in this study, however, you have a good start. You've actually begun to create a new discipline in your lives.

5. Why is it so difficult to make your spiritual lives together a priority?

6. If you were to pray together and study the Bible together more consistently, how do you think it would affect your marriage? What are some practical ways to pray and study the Bible as a couple?

7. Read James 1:22–25. How does this passage relate to our taking action on what we know God wants us to do in our marriages?

8. How has your spiritual intimacy improved as you've completed the HomeBuilders projects? What can you do to continue this new discipline in your lives?

PICTURE THIS

Spread out as much as possible in your meeting area, but stay with your spouse. Stand side by side with your spouse, facing the same direction, and move about three feet apart. Place one of your books on the floor several steps in front of you. Then listen as your leader reads the following descriptive statements. After each statement, both of you take one small step toward your book.

- You maintain a regular personal quiet time and share insights with your spouse.
- You share together how a sermon affected you.
- You pray together.
- You apply the Bible's principles to your personal life and marriage.
- You seek God's will in your decisions.

Discuss the following questions in your group:
- What happened to the distance between you and your spouse as you moved toward your book?
- How is this like what happens when you seek to draw closer to God in your lives and marriages?
- If you did what the statements said, what difference would it make in the communication in your marriage?

9. What types of things are likely to prevent your continuing this discipline? What can you do to keep your commitment from falling by the wayside?

homebuilders principle: You can grow the spiritual intimacy in your marriage by regularly praying and studying the Bible together.

make a date

Set a time for you and your spouse to complete the last HomeBuilders project of the study.

date _____ time _____

location _____

homebuilders project

Complete this project together. Purpose to continue your habit of taking one evening each week to study the Bible together, just as you've worked on the HomeBuilders projects during this course. If you need help finding a resource for further Bible study as a couple, talk to your group leader or pastor.

1 Corinthians 13

Read the scripture passage together, and then answer the questions. Talk about what you can do in your day-to-day relationship to strengthen your marriage and family through what you learn from God's Word. Pray together that God will help you follow through on strengthening your marriage.

1. First Corinthians 13 is often referred to as the love chapter. As you read it, how do you feel about the different descriptions of love? How well have you demonstrated them in your relationship with your spouse?

2. How would you contrast our culture's messages about love with this passage's message?

3. What impresses you most about this passage? Which of these principles have you seen your spouse embody in some way?

4. Verse 8 tells us, "Love never ends" or "never fails" (NIV). What do you need to do in your relationship to strengthen the never-failing love that God wants for your marriage?

5. Look through all the descriptions of love. In what area do you most need to change to show God-honoring love to your spouse?

where do you go from here?

We hope that you have benefited from this study in the Home-Builders Couples Series and that your marriage will continue to grow as you both submit your lives to Jesus Christ and build according to his blueprints. We also hope that you will reach out to strengthen other marriages in your local church and community. Your influence is needed.

A favorite World War II story illustrates this point clearly.

The year was 1940. The French army had just collapsed under Hitler's onslaught. The Dutch had folded, overwhelmed by the Nazi regime. The Belgians had surrendered. And the British army was trapped on the coast of France in the channel port of Dunkirk.

Two hundred twenty thousand of Britain's finest young men seemed doomed to die, turning the English Channel red with their blood. The Fuehrer's troops, only miles away in the hills of France, didn't realize how close to victory they actually were.

Any attempt at rescue seemed futile in the time remaining. A thin British navy—the professionals—told King George VI that they could save 17,000 troops at best. The House of Commons was warned to prepare for "hard and heavy tidings."

Politicians were paralyzed. The king was powerless. And the Allies could only watch as spectators from a distance. Then as the doom of the British army seemed imminent, a strange fleet appeared on the horizon of the English Channel—the wildest assortment of boats perhaps ever assembled in history. Trawlers, tugs, scows, fishing sloops, lifeboats, pleasure craft, smacks and coasters, sailboats, even the London fire-brigade flotilla. Ships manned by civilian volunteers—English fathers joining in the rescue of Britain's exhausted, bleeding sons.

William Manchester writes in his epic novel *The Last Lion* that what happened in 1940 at Dunkirk seems like a miracle. Not only were most of the British soldiers rescued but 118,000 other Allied troops as well.

Today the Christian home is much like those troops at Dunkirk—pressured, trapped, demoralized, and in need of help. The Christian community may be much like England—waiting for professionals to step in and save the family. But the problem is much too large for them to solve alone.

We need an all-out effort by men and women "sailing" to rescue the exhausted and wounded families. We need an outreach effort by common couples with faith in an uncommon God. For too long, married couples within the church have abdicated to those in full-time vocational ministry the privilege and responsibility of influencing others.

We challenge you to invest your lives in others, to join in the rescue. You and other couples around the world can team together to build thousands of marriages and families and, in doing so, continue to strengthen your own.

Be a HomeBuilder

Here are some practical ways you can make a difference in families today:

- Gather a group of four to seven couples and lead them through this HomeBuilders study. Consider challenging others in your church or community to form additional HomeBuilders groups.
- Commit to continue building marriages by doing another small-group study in the HomeBuilders Couples Series®.
- Consider using the *JESUS* film as an outreach. For more information contact FamilyLife at the number or website below.
- Host a dinner party. Invite families from your neighborhood to your home, and as a couple share your faith in Christ.
- If you have attended FamilyLife's Weekend to Remember® marriage getaway, consider offering to assist your pastor in counseling engaged couples, using the material you received.

For more information about these ministry opportunities, contact your local church or

FamilyLife
PO Box 7111
Little Rock, AR 72223
1-800-FL-TODAY
FamilyLife.com

Every couple has to deal with problems in marriage—communication problems, money problems, difficulties with sexual intimacy, and more. Learning how to handle these issues is important to cultivating a strong and loving relationship.

The Big Problem

One basic problem is at the heart of every other problem in marriage, and it's too big for any person to deal with on his or her own. The problem is separation from God. If you want to experience life and marriage the way they were designed to be, you need a vital relationship with the God who created you.

But sin separates us from God. Some try to deal with sin by working hard to become better people. They may read books on how to control anger, or they may resolve to stop cheating on their taxes, but in their hearts they know—we all know—that the sin problem runs much deeper than bad habits and will take more than our best behavior to overcome it. In reality, we have rebelled against God. We have ignored him and have decided to run our lives in a way that makes sense to us, thinking that our ideas and plans are better than his.

> For all have sinned and fall short of the glory of God.
> (Romans 3:23)

What does it mean to "fall short of the glory of God"? It means that none of us has trusted and treasured God the way we should. We have sought to satisfy ourselves with other things and have treated them as more valuable than God. We have gone our own way. According to the Bible, we have to pay a penalty for our sin. We cannot simply do things the way we choose and hope it will be okay with God. Following our own plans leads to our destruction.

> There is a way that seems right to a man, but its end
> is the way to death. (Proverbs 14:12)

> For the wages of sin is death. (Romans 6:23)

The penalty for sin is that we are separated from God's love. God is holy, and we are sinful. No matter how hard we try, we cannot come up with some plan, like living a good life or even trying to do what the Bible says, and hope that we can avoid the penalty.

God's Solution to Sin

Thankfully, God has a way to solve our dilemma. He became a man through the person of Jesus Christ. Jesus lived a holy life in perfect obedience to God's plan. He also willingly died on a cross to pay our penalty for sin. Then he proved that he is more powerful than sin or death by rising from the dead. He alone has the power to overrule the penalty for our sin.

> Jesus said to him, "I am the way, and the truth, and the
> life. No one comes to the Father except through me."
> (John 14:6)

But God shows his love for us in that while we were still sinners, Christ died for us. (Romans 5:8)

For the wages of sin is death, but the free gift of God is eternal life in Christ Jesus our Lord. (Romans 6:23)

The death and resurrection of Jesus have fixed our sin problem. He has bridged the gap between God and us. He is calling us to come to him and to give up our flawed plans for running our lives. He wants us to trust God and his plan.

Accepting God's Solution

If you recognize that you are separated from God, he is calling you to confess your sins. All of us have made messes of our lives because we have stubbornly preferred our ideas and plans to his. As a result, we deserve to be cut off from God's love and his care for us. But God has promised that if we will acknowledge that we have rebelled against his plan, he will forgive us and will fix our sin problem.

But to all who did receive him, who believed in his name, he gave the right to become children of God. (John 1:12)

For by grace you have been saved through faith. And this is not your own doing; it is the gift of God, not a result of works, so that no one may boast. (Ephesians 2:8–9)

When the Bible talks about receiving Christ, it means we acknowledge that we are sinners and that we can't fix the problem ourselves. It means we turn away from our sin. And it means we trust Christ to forgive our sins and to make us the kind of people he wants us to be. It's not enough to intellectually believe that Christ is the Son of God. We must trust in him and his plan for our lives by faith, as an act of the will.

Are things right between you and God, with him and his plan at the center of your life? Or is life spinning out of control as you seek to make your own way?

If you have been trying to make your own way, you can decide today to change. You can turn to Christ and allow him to transform your life. All you need to do is talk to him and tell him what is stirring in your mind and in your heart. If you've never done this, consider taking the steps listed here:

- Do you agree that you need God? Tell God.
- Have you made a mess of your life by following your own plan? Tell God.
- Do you want God to forgive you? Tell God.
- Do you believe that Jesus' death on the cross and his resurrection from the dead gave him the power to fix your sin problem and to grant you the free gift of eternal life? Tell God.
- Are you ready to acknowledge that God's plan for your life is better than any plan you could come up with? Tell God.
- Do you agree that God has the right to be the Lord and Master of your life? Tell God.

Seek the LORD while he may be found; call upon him while he is near. (Isaiah 55:6)

Here is a suggested prayer:

Lord Jesus, I need you. Thank you for dying on the cross for my sins. I receive you as my Savior and Lord. Thank you for forgiving my sins and giving me eternal life. Make me the kind of person you want me to be.

The Christian Life

For the person who is a follower of Christ—a Christian—the penalty for sin is paid in full. But the effect of sin continues throughout our lives.

> If we say we have no sin, we deceive ourselves, and the truth is not in us. (1 John 1:8)

> For I do not do the good I want, but the evil I do not want is what I keep on doing. (Romans 7:19)

The effects of sin carry over into our marriages as well. Even Christians struggle to maintain solid, God-honoring marriages. Most couples eventually realize they can't do it on their own. But with God's help, they can succeed.

To learn more, read the extended version of this article at FamilyLife.com/Resources.

leader's notes

What is the leader's job?

Your role is more of a facilitator than a teacher. A teacher usually does most of the talking and instructing whereas a facilitator encourages people to think and to discover what Scripture says. You should help group members feel comfortable and keep things moving forward.

Is there a structure to the sessions?

Yes, each session is composed of the following categories:

Warm-Up (5–10 minutes): The purpose of Warm-Up is to help people unwind from a busy day and get to know one another better. Typically the Warm-Up starts with an exercise that is fun but also introduces the topic of the session.

Blueprints (45–50 minutes): This is the heart of the study when people answer questions related to the topic of study and look to God's Word for understanding. Some of the questions are to be discussed between spouses and others with the whole group.

HomeBuilders Project (60 minutes): This project is the unique application that couples will work on between the group meetings. Each HomeBuilders project contains two sections: (1) On your own—questions for husbands and wives to answer individually and (2) With your spouse—an opportunity for couples to share their answers with each other and to make application in their lives.

In addition to these regular features, occasional activities are labeled "Picture This." These activities provide a more active or visual way to make a particular point.

What is the best setting and time schedule for this study?

This study is designed as a small-group, home Bible study. However, it can be adapted for more structured settings like a Sunday school class. Here are some suggestions for using this study in various settings:

In a small group

To create a friendly and comfortable atmosphere, we recommend you do this study in a home setting. In many cases the couple that leads the study also serves as host, but sometimes involving another couple as host is a good idea. Choose the option you believe will work best for your group, taking into account factors such as the number of couples participating and the location.

Each session is designed as a sixty-minute study, but we recommend a ninety-minute block of time to allow for more relaxed conversation and refreshments. Be sure to keep in mind one of the cardinal rules of a small group: good groups start *and* end on time. People's time is valuable, and your group will appreciate your respecting this.

In a Sunday school class

If you want to use the study in a class setting, you need to adapt it in two important ways: (1) You should focus on the content of the Blueprints section of each session. That is the heart of the session.

(2) Many Sunday school classes use a teacher format instead of a small-group format. If this study is used in a class setting, the class should adapt to a small-group dynamic. This will involve an interactive, discussion-based format and may also require a class to break into multiple smaller groups.

What is the best size group?

We recommend from four to seven couples (including you and your spouse). If more people are interested than you can accommodate, consider asking someone to lead a second group. If you have a large group, you may find it beneficial to break into smaller subgroups on occasion. This helps you cover the material in a timely fashion and allows for optimum interaction and participation within the group.

What about refreshments?

Many groups choose to serve refreshments, which helps create an environment of fellowship. If you plan to include refreshments, here are a couple of suggestions: (1) For the first session (or two) you should provide the refreshments. Then involve the group by having people sign up to bring them on later dates. (2) Consider starting your group with a short time of informal fellowship and refreshments (15–20 minutes). Then move into the study. If couples are late, they miss only the food and don't disrupt the study. You may also want to have refreshments available again at the end of your meeting to encourage fellowship. But remember to respect the group members' time by ending the session on schedule and allowing anyone who needs to leave to do so gracefully.

What about child care?

Groups handle this differently, depending on their needs. Here are a couple of options you may want to consider:

- Have people be responsible for making their own arrangements.
- As a group, hire someone to provide child care, and have all the children watched in one location.

What about prayer?

An important part of a small group is prayer. However, as the leader, you need to be sensitive to people's comfort level with praying in front of others. Never call on people to pray aloud unless you know they are comfortable doing this. You can take creative approaches, such as modeling prayer, calling for volunteers, and letting people state their prayers in the form of finishing a sentence. A helpful tool in a group is a prayer list. You should lead the prayer time, but allow another couple to create, update, and distribute prayer lists as their ministry to the group.

Find additional help and suggestions for leading your HomeBuilders group at FamilyLife.com/Resources.

about the leader's notes

The sessions in this study can be easily led without a lot of preparation time. However, accompanying Leader's Notes have been provided to assist you when needed. The categories within the Leader's Notes are as follows:

Objectives

The Objectives focus on the issues that will be presented in each session.

Notes and Tips

This section provides general ideas, helps, and suggestions about the session. You may want to create a checklist of things to include in each session.

Blueprints Commentary

This section contains notes that relate to the Blueprints questions. Not all Blueprints questions will have accompanying commentary notes. The number of the commentary note corresponds to the number of the question it relates to. (For example, the Leader's Notes, session 1, number 5 in the Blueprints Commentary section relates back to session 1, Blueprints, question 5.)

session one

understanding the barriers to communication

Objectives

Building a healthy marriage requires strong communication; strong communication requires an understanding of the things that interfere.

In this session couples will

- discuss why communication is so vital to a marriage,
- examine barriers to communication, and
- look at some initial steps to overcoming those barriers.

Notes and Tips

1. If you have not already done so, you will want to read the information "About Leading a HomeBuilders Group," and "About the Leader's Notes," starting on page 77.

2. As part of the first session, you may want to review with the group some ground rules (see page ix in Welcome to HomeBuilders).

3. At this first meeting collect the names, phone numbers, and e-mail addresses of the group members. You may want to make a list that you can copy and distribute to the entire group.

4. Because this is the first session, make a special point to tell the group about the importance of the HomeBuilders project. Encourage each couple to make a date for a time before the next meeting to complete the project. Mention that you will ask about this during Warm-Up at the next session.

5. You may want to offer a closing prayer instead of asking others to pray aloud. Many people are uncomfortable praying in front of others, and unless you already know your group well, it may be wise to venture slowly into various methods of prayer. Regardless of how you decide to close, you should serve as a model.

6. If there is room for more people, you may want to remind the group that they can still invite another couple to join them since the study is just under way.

7. The key in this week's study is to raise the awareness of each couple that it is natural to have barriers; we just need to determine what they are and then develop a plan to overcome them. Some couples may feel uneasy, wondering, "Can I trust these people?" Encourage everyone that you are a team and you are all working on sharpening your skills.

8. Consider using the following activity after question 3 in the Blueprints section as a way to illustrate communication barriers. Prior to asking question 4, say, "Before we move on, I'm going to try a little experiment," then turn on a

television or some music. Be sure the volume is loud enough to make conversation difficult. Begin discussing question 4 as normally as possible. Then ask: "How does it make you feel to try to talk to one another over the noise? What does this teach us about dealing with the barriers to communication?"

Blueprints Commentary

Here is some additional information about various Blueprints questions. (Note: the numbers below correspond to the Blueprints questions they relate to.) If you share any of these points, do so in a manner that does not stifle discussion by making you the authority with the real answers. Begin your comments by saying things like, "One thing I notice in this passage is . . ." or, "I think another reason for this is . . ."

1. Many couples never receive training in how to communicate with each other. They may not have had a good model as they grew up, and they perhaps haven't learned communication skills. Consequently, they don't understand the differences between themselves and their spouses—or even the general differences between men and women. They feel a distance and don't know how to talk about it or solve their problem.

2. Communication is the lifeblood of a marriage relationship. Effective communication helps us avoid problems. It is the key to harmony in marriage.

3. Men generally do not communicate their emotions as readily as women. They tend to communicate facts and opinions and prefer to get to the bottom line of a discussion rather than connect emotionally. Men's comments tend to be short and to the point, and women often want more detail.

   Be sure to keep the discussion focused on the differing communication styles of men and women. Some may want to discuss whether men and women are born with these differences or whether they are learned behaviors, but that is not a critical issue for this discussion.

7. Martha was too concerned with all the work that needed to be done and forgot that her greatest priority should be to listen to Jesus. While her intent was to serve, her priorities were misplaced.

9. It's important to speak the truth, but love can influence how you do that. If you speak truth without love, for example, you may alienate or discourage others by your insensitivity.

session two

making your relationship a priority

Objectives

To develop positive communication patterns, you must make your marriage relationship a priority.

In this session couples will

- examine the need to make their relationship a high priority,
- learn practical ways to set priorities, and
- apply these principles to their marriages.

Notes and Tips

1. Since this is the second session, your group members have probably warmed up a bit to one another but may not yet feel free to be completely open and honest about their relationships. Don't force the issue, but continue encouraging couples to attend and to complete their projects.

2. You may wish to have extra study guides and Bibles available for those who come to the session without them.

3. If someone joins the group for the first time in this session, give a brief summary of the main points of session 1. Also be sure to introduce people who do not know each other. You may want to have each new couple answer the Warm-Up question from session 1.

4. If refreshments are planned for this session, make sure arrangements for them have been made.

5. If your group has decided to use a prayer list, make sure this is covered.

6. The Warm-Up in this session takes a lighthearted look at communication problems within a marriage. Encourage people to have fun with it. As they do, they'll track real communication problems without having to reveal any of their own issues.

7. If you told the group during the first session that you'd be asking them to share something they learned from the first HomeBuilders project, be sure to ask them. This is an important way for you to establish an environment of accountability.

8. You may want to ask for a volunteer or two to close the session in prayer. Check ahead of time with a couple of people you think might be comfortable praying aloud.

Blueprints Commentary

2.

- Ephesians 5:15–16—You will strive to use time wisely and not waste it on things that are unimportant.
- Philippians 2:1–4—You will be mindful of others and their needs when making decisions about how to use your time.
- Song of Solomon 7:10–13—As a couple you delight in each other, desire each other, and make time for just the two of you.

3. If people have trouble coming up with examples, share the following:

Each weekday evening my dad arrived home from work around 5:30. The four kids would run to greet him, and then he would sit down with my mom and talk for about an hour. What did they talk about? The business. The children. Their relationship. We kids knew we weren't invited, and believe me, we didn't want to be there. But occasionally I would go into the kitchen and watch them through the doorway. I recall some pretty serious times when they were dealing with problems in the family business. I remember other times of laughter or true emotional intimacy. But they always talked.

Today, Barb and I are following their example. The first thing we do each day when I come home from work is head into the living room and talk. We look forward to it each day, and it sets the mood for the rest of the evening. It's an oasis in a hectic day.

6. This may be a difficult issue for some people to confront, because in many cases it means cutting back on activities they enjoy or on responsibilities they have committed to. For some, it may mean not working as many hours or not bringing work home as often. Others may have to choose not to pursue promotions, raises, or new job opportunities. Some may have to cut back on time spent with hobbies or other outside activities. For others, it could mean making a conscious effort to put the same type of effort and creativity into their families as their jobs, even if they can't give as much.

session three

communication 101

Objectives

Learning to use basic communication skills will enhance understanding within your marriage.

In this session couples will

- discuss three basic components of communication, and
- apply these concepts to their marriages.

Notes and Tips

1. Congratulations. With the completion of this session, you will be halfway through this study. It's time for a checkup: How are you feeling? How is the group going? What has worked well so far? What things would you consider changing as you head into the second half?

2. In this session we look at some basics of communication. For some couples this may be old information, while for others it will at least be a reminder of skills that need to be sharpened. This is simply a time to identify areas to begin working on, not a time to make radical changes.

3. This session includes quite a few principles that may seem basic, but consistently practicing them in marriage can be

difficult. Any couple with serious communication problems probably struggles with the principles you'll discuss in this session.

4. Remember the importance of starting and ending on time.

5. You may find it helpful to make some notes right after the meeting so you can evaluate how things went. Ask yourself questions like: Did everyone participate? Is there anyone I should make a special effort to follow up with before the next session?

6. As a model to the group, you should complete the Home-Builders projects.

Blueprints Commentary

2. The tongue can't be tamed. It wields power much like a bit directs a horse or a rudder guides a ship. Like a fire, it spreads its influence to all areas.

3. You might want to mention the Warm-Up question in which the group members told what attracted them to their spouses. Ask, "How do you feel when you hear your spouse talk about things that are attractive to him or to her?"

4. Many of us prefer to talk rather than listen. It's hard not to interrupt with comments or feedback. We may get busy, impatient, distracted, disinterested, or selfish. Or we may

become so preoccupied with the issues in our own lives that we don't take time to think of another person.

8. Mention the following only if your group has trouble coming up with responses: ridiculing what your spouse says; shrugging off what he or she says as if it doesn't matter; talking too much yourself; becoming defensive; being too analytical; trying to find a solution too quickly; changing the subject.

9. Again, suggest the following only if your group has trouble coming up with a good list: giving your spouse your full attention; making good eye contact; allowing your spouse to speak without interruption; asking probing and uncritical questions to draw your spouse out; giving appropriate touch; showing empathy; being approachable.

   Feedback can consist of clarifying questions such as, "What did you mean when you said . . ." Summary questions are also valuable: "Of all that you just said, what do you most want me to understand?"

session four

closing the loop in conflict

Objectives

Resolving conflict requires taking initiative to mend the relationship.
In this session couples will

- understand that conflict is inevitable in marriage,
- discuss their need to make a conscious effort to resolve
  a conflict once it begins,
- discuss four steps in resolving conflict, and
- apply these principles to their marriages.

Notes and Tips

1. We've found that the very act of discussing conflict sometimes *causes* conflict. As group leader, you must set a
   relaxed and accepting atmosphere, and the Warm-Up
   should help you.

2. The primary focus of this session is the need for couples to
   make an effort to resolve conflict. The last part of this session
   introduces a biblical pattern for resolving conflict that we call
   "closing the loop." We recommend you read the material in
   session 4 before leading this session so you will understand
   the entire process of closing the loop.

3. Conflict is a part of every relationship. The process of closing the loop was developed in counseling sessions with hundreds of couples, just like those in your study, who needed to learn how to get through times of conflict. Tell your group members that this process is a tool that can help resolve conflict. Encourage them to try it out. You might want to pick up a copy of *Dr. Rosberg's Do-It-Yourself Relationship Mender* for a comprehensive look at how this process works.

4. As you talk about preparing hearts during the closing the loop process, remind couples how important it is to bring God into the midst of their communication. Prayer and Bible study can help greatly in resolving our conflicts.

5. The offering of forgiveness that we will talk about today is key in healing hurts. God's plan is to bring these times of forgiveness into our marriages.

6. By this time group members should be more comfortable with one another. At the end of this session, you may want to give everyone an opportunity to pray by asking the group to finish a sentence that starts something like this: *"Lord, I want to thank you for _____."* Be sensitive to those who are not comfortable doing this.

Blueprints Commentary

1. If your group has trouble coming up with ideas, suggest the following: lack of communication, different perspectives of conflict, a tendency to avoid conflict, lack of good role models growing up, poor role models in the media.

3. Anger often prevents conflicts from being resolved peacefully. Either angry feelings are expressed with hostility and pain—as a weapon—or they are buried deep within the heart, allowing bitterness and resentment to grow. True intimacy will never be experienced until the loop is closed.

4. Some factors are pride, guilt, laziness, fear, anger, hurt feelings, fatigue, and ignorance of how to resolve conflict. For example, pride can keep a person from taking the initiative to resolve a conflict, rationalizing that the other person should humble himself or herself first.

6. Ephesians 4:26–27—When you "let the sun go down on your anger," you are choosing to harbor that anger in your heart rather than attempting to resolve the conflict. You need to resolve conflicts quickly; otherwise that suppressed anger will allow bitterness to take root in your heart.

7. If you enter a conflict seeking to win or to prove the other person wrong, you will only make matters worse. These scriptures call for humility and setting aside the desire for revenge.

9. God was so concerned about resolving the "conflict" that existed between him and his creation that he made the greatest possible sacrifice to offer forgiveness. That's the kind of forgiveness we're to show others, including our spouses.

session five

communicating through the trials of life

Objectives

God can use you to encourage your spouse during times of trial.
In this session couples will

- think about the trials they have already experienced,
- discuss their need to turn to God for strength, and
- discover how they can encourage each other and improve
  communication during trials.

Notes and Tips

1. This session will help couples acknowledge that trials are
   inevitable. Many marriages struggle or collapse because
   the couples are unable to withstand trials in their lives.
   Humans don't like thinking about problems and trials,
   and as a result, many couples turn away from each other
   rather than cling to each other for strength.

2. Some couples, as they work through this session, will
   think, "We don't have many problems . . . we are blessed."
   Others will hear couples talk about their trials and think,
   "Is that all they worry about? Boy, are *we* in trouble!"

Encourage the couples to realize that everyone has different needs, and none is insignificant.

3. During times of loss, trials may seem unbearable. During times of major change, people may feel they'll never get through it. If people in your group are struggling with major trials, be sensitive to their needs and remind them that God will sustain them.

4. If you have a regular prayer time at the end of your session, ask couples to share what trials they're currently facing so the group can pray together about them. This will help bond the group and demonstrate how encouragement from other people can help during trials.

5. As the leader of a small group, you can play a vital role by praying specifically for each member. Why not take some time to do this as you prepare for this session?

Blueprints Commentary

1. One problem is that many of us don't have the right attitude about trials. We know that we'll face trials, but we would rather not think about the pain they'll bring. Also, many of us simply don't know how to deal with trials when they come.

2. With some couples, trials drive them toward each other and toward a greater dependency upon God. With many others,

trials intensify any pressure they already are feeling in the relationship. Trials may drive a wedge between a husband and wife if they deal with the problems on their own rather than together.

6. Note that each passage presents part of God's perspective about our trials. God uses them for our good (Romans 8:28), they test our faith and cause us to glorify Christ as we maintain our love for him (1 Peter 1:3–9), and he gives us his Spirit as a blessing (1 Peter 4:12–14).

8. First Corinthians 10:13 and Philippians 4:12–13 assure us that God provides the strength we need to handle any situation. (It's interesting to note that Paul was in prison when he wrote Philippians.) Second Corinthians 1:3–4 assures us of God's comfort during trials.

9. Rejoicing in God despite suffering demonstrates your belief in God's sovereignty. Praying demonstrates your dependence on God and your belief that he will respond.

session six

achieving spiritual intimacy

Objectives

The best and deepest level of communication is achieved when you seek God together.

In this session couples will

- consider the need to seek God together in their marriage,
- evaluate their present level of spiritual intimacy, and
- make plans to continue working on spiritual intimacy as they have during this study.

Notes and Tips

1. This session presents the key to the entire area of marital communication: Marriage is a relationship of three, not two. Compromise really isn't the answer; obedience to God is. When both the man and the woman are growing in their vertical relationships with God, the horizontal relationship between them comes together as well. This session draws on God's Word to show how important it is to be of one heart and one mind in marriage. Not only one with each other but also with God.

2. While this HomeBuilders Couples Series has great value, people are likely to gradually return to previous patterns

of living unless they commit to a plan for continuing the progress they've made. During this final session, encourage couples to take specific steps beyond this series to keep their marriages growing. For example, you may want to challenge couples who have developed the habit of a date night during the course to continue this practice. Also, you may want the group to consider doing another study from this series.

3. The final HomeBuilders project encourages couples to study the Bible together. You may want to emphasize the value of this by offering to help them find resources for continuing their Bible study.

Blueprints Commentary

3. Suggest some of the following if your group doesn't come up with something similar: We would clothe ourselves with compassion, kindness, humility, meekness, and patience. We would bear with each other and forgive each other. We would "put on love." We would do everything to please Jesus. Such attitudes and actions couldn't help but improve our marriage relationships.

4. It's important to regularly point each other to God. We've done this in our marriage by praying together, for example. And we've communicated with each other about what God is doing in our lives. From early in our Christian experience, we've asked each other, "Tell me what you are learning." This has begun rich, intimate conversations that have knit our hearts together.

5. One reason is that many couples allow their time to be filled with other pursuits: hobbies, family activities, entertainment, etc. Another typical reason is that spouses wait for the other to take the lead in this area. Also, it's important to realize that this is a spiritual battle; Satan wants to keep you from doing the one thing that will cement your relationship more than anything else.

6. These two actions may be the most important disciplines a couple can build into their marriage. It will revolutionize their relationship because they will draw closer to each other as they draw closer to God.

more tools for leaders

Looking for more ways to help people build their marriages and families?

Thank you for your efforts to help people develop their marriages and families using biblical principles. We recognize the influence that one person—or couple—can have on another, and we'd like to help you multiply your ministry.

FamilyLife is pleased to offer a wide range of resources in various formats. Visit us online at FamilyLife.com, where you will find information about our:

- getaways and events, featuring Weekend to Remember® and The Art of Marrige® offered in cities throughout the United States;
- multimedia resources for small groups, churches, and community networking;
- interactive products for parents, couples, small-group leaders, and one-to-one mentors; and
- assortment of blogs, forums, and other online connections.

FamilyLife is a nonprofit, Christian organization focused on the mission of helping every home become a godly home. Believing that family is the foundation of society, FamilyLife works in more than a hundred countries around the world to build healthier marriages and families through marriage getaways and events, small-group curriculum, *FamilyLife Today*® radio broadcasts, Hope for Orphans® orphan care ministry, the Internet, and a wide range of marriage and family resources.

Dennis Rainey is the president and CEO of FamilyLife (a ministry of Campus Crusade for Christ known as Cru in the United States) and a graduate of Dallas Theological Seminary. For more than thirty-five years, he has been speaking and writing on marriage and family issues. Since 1976, he has overseen the development of FamilyLife's numerous outreaches, including the popular Weekend to Remember® marriage getaway. He is also the daily host of the nationally syndicated radio program *FamilyLife Today*. Barbara is an artist and author. Her books include *Thanksgiving: A Time to Remember*, *Barbara and Susan's Guide to the Empty Nest*, and *When Christmas Came*. The Raineys have six children and numerous grandchildren.